The Adventures of
Pumpkin Jackson

By

Glenda Faison-Crawford

Welstar Publications
New York

THE ADVENTURES OF PUMPKIN JACKSON

GLENDA
FAISON-CRAWFORD

Written by Glenda Faison-Crawford
Published by Welstar Publications, LLC.
Horace Batson, Ph.D., Publisher
628 Lexington Avenue, Brooklyn, NY 11221.
Phone: (646) 409-0340
Fax: (313) 453-6554
E-mail: drbatson@optonline.net
ISBN: 978-0-938503-30-9

Managing Editor, Horace Batson, PhD
Transcription: Carlo Craig
Book Design/Typography, Lori Monroe
Text set in Calisto MT

DEDICATION

This book is dedicated to the

"Youth"

who need a voice!

THE ADVENTURES OF
PUMPKIN JACKSON

Table of Contents

i

Foreword

To God be the glory!
Good for you Pumpkin,
good you stood your ground!

When you think of bullies, we think of the traditional bully: some loud, big person making threats at smaller, weaker people, but with all the social media; text, twitter, video, all the daily drama from the lives of young people-all the rumors of "he said, she said," the threats, being attacked verbally or physically, cyber bullying- Bullying of all types happens anytime, anywhere, to anyone for whatever reason.

There was bullying in the Bible! Joseph's big brothers, Pharaoh and Goliath just to name a few.

"The Challengers" lived up to their name. The sad thing is that they did not view their attitudes and behavior as bullying. The jokes and games-as innocent as they start out can be mean and hurting. Some emotional wounds never heal and last even into adulthood.

Thank God for the family and friends support because Pumpkin stood up! Spoke up! The problem was dealt with and solved.

Glenda, my grandchildren enjoyed the reading and we had a discussion afterwards.

This is an excellent discussion starter for tweens and teens and even the younger age group that can be used in youth workshops and Bible classes.

Thank you for sharing and reminding us that no matter who you are, that you can go to your parents or persons in charge and talk things over. As long as you are afraid and silent, the abuse will continue...may we all encourage our children in love not to be afraid, to speak up and speak out.

Be Blessed.
Rev. Sara Streeter-McRae

Acknowledgments

Because "It takes a village to raise a child" there is no way I could have done this book without the love, devotion, rearing and childhood memories of my parents, Billy and Betty Faison, my brothers Eugene and Christopher Faison (who tortured me but made me laugh constantly), to my brother Kenneth, "Thank you."

To my high school friends from Bamberg American High School, Bamberg, Germany (1980-1982) especially Shon Malone, Fort Knox High School (Class of 1985) - especially my history teacher, Ms. Felice Wahlberg and the countless other friends that I met along the way living the military family life.

To my best friend Alyce Mauldin, who is there at the drop of a dime for me. To my cousin Shamika Ashley, who is more like a sister and her daughters are mine. Thanks to my nieces, Ta'Nesha & Amesha Jackson, for critiquing the book through the eyes of honest youth and to their mother LaCaroll. To my extended family, Mother-n-Law Ruby Crawford, Sisters-n-Law's Sylvia & Cynthia Crawford, and Brother-n-Law Timothy Crawford, "You are truly wonderful and supportive in every way!

Much appreciation to Rev. Sara Streeter-McCrae for whom I teach Christian Education under (lesson plans have strengthened my creativity like you wouldn't believe) and Rev. Ella Medley, who wouldn't settle for anything less than, "Your Best!" at Community Bible Institute. To our daughter's God Parents, Pastor & First Lady, Harry Brown and a heartfelt commendation to my Pastor and First Lady, The Rev. Dr. and Mrs. Bruce Davis, Sr. for teaching me to, "Stretch My Faith!"

A standing ovation goes to my aunt Lula "Liz" Miller, who has gone on to be with the Lord - but her wisdom shall never cease. To my cousin Junuis, "Thank you!" Many hugs to First Lady Theresa Whitfield, who chose to bless me with the knowledge of Welstar Publications, LLC and to you, Dr. Horace Batson, for giving me the chance. Praise goes to the Ebenezer Youth Liturgical Dancers, who are there for me whenever I need them or their community. They continue to be a blessing.

Last but not least, an applause goes to my wonderful husband, Vincent Crawford, who has pushed me to, "Get the job done!" and our daughter Alexandria Egypt Crawford, our gift from God. I love you both very much!

Glenda Faison-Crawford

Introduction

I was an only child for ten years so I had to exercise my imagination at an early age. I began sewing doll clothes at the age of nine years old when my mom gave me some scraps of old jeans. She told me that we couldn't afford to buy my Barbie dolls clothing every week. She gave me a needle and thread and told me to make them! So I did, for myself and my friends!

My dad has always been proud of his military career in The United States Army of twenty-nine years. He taught us to take pride in whatever we create and set forth to do.

I began writing love stories in English literature class, in the tenth grade and passing them out to my friends. By the next period they were hooked and wanted to know what was going to happen next.

My husband and I got married October 9, 2004. I awoke very early one morning and asked God to give me a theme for our wedding. As I went to the store I found some beautiful baskets that were in the shape of pumpkins made out of banana leaves. So we had an autumn theme. On my birthday October 25th of that particular year, my husband sent me a beautiful floral bouquet of autumn flowers in a ceramic pot shaped like a pumpkin. As I picked up my flowers in the front office at work, the Lord spoke to me and said, "Your character will have the name, Pumpkin Jackson!"

Thank you, Jesus, for your love, guidance and the power of God's Holy Spirit! I'm so glad I stepped out on faith and listened.

The Adventures of
Pumpkin Jackson

Chapter 1

Introducing Pumpkin

Hello! You don't know me but my name is Pumpkin Jackson. That's right-Pumpkin Jackson! I'm sitting in the principal's office, and no, I'm not in trouble. It's my first day of school at Memorial Park Elementary in Fort Jake, New York. I'm an official "Army Brat." My father is a drill sergeant, as he would proudly boast, "In the United States Army." My mother is a hair stylist and I have a one-year-old baby brother named Elisha. He is spoiled rotten to the core!

The principal is a short, plump, African-American woman named Mrs. Fletcher. She has a smile that reminds me of my grandma's. Her hair is jet black and curled extremely tight. *I bet my mom will comment on that later.* "Mr. and Mrs. Jackson, I'm truly impressed with Pumpkin's school records. It seems as if she's right on track with our curriculum. She will be placed in Mrs. Carson's fifth grade class."

My parents are sitting here with these goofy grins on their faces. I'm just happy for once in my ten years of life that I don't have to go through ten million tests to see if I'm up to this school's standards. *Mrs. Carson.* I hope she's nice. My last teacher in Kentucky was pretty cool. We are originally from New York, so my parents were so excited when our military orders came in for Fort Jake.

"Pumpkin, are you ready to meet your teacher?" Mrs. Fletcher asked. "Yes, Mrs. Fletcher," I responded. Mrs. Fletcher is babbling on and on to my parents about the other programs the school offers. I know I should be listening but my stomach is in knots. I have been through this scenario plenty of times. Just picture this in your head-I'm about to walk into a classroom full of kids that I don't even know. Everyone is going to stop what they're doing. The principal will introduce my parents to the new teacher who has been expecting me. The teacher will smile and shake my hand, and then she will turn her head to the classroom and part her lips. *"May I please have everyone's attention? I would like to introduce you to our new student, Pum..."*

"Girl, stop day-dreaming and stand up straight," my mother warned. I rubbed my shoulder from her pinch as we were about to enter the classroom. "Yes, Mom." "Here it goes," I whispered to myself. "Good morning, everyone." "Good morning, Mrs. Flet-cher." *Don't you just hate having to say an adult's name the same way you have since Kindergarten? Oops, I'm sorry-I'm not supposed to be day-dreaming.*

"I would like to introduce Mr. and Mrs. Jackson to all of you. Would you please welcome them?" Mrs. Fletcher requested. *Wow, that's different.* Both of my parents shook Mrs. Carson's hand. The class said hello and silence fell. "Now, I would like for everyone to please show your new classmate what makes Memorial Park Elementary one of the top schools in our area. Please welcome your new friend, Pumpkin Jackson," said Mrs. Carson. *Laughter, laughter, laughter! Oh yeah, I heard a couple of "hello's."*

Mrs. Carson-who by the way is absolutely beautiful-gave me a hearty hand shake. My parents looked down and gave me a smile and that, "You-be-proud-of-your-name" look. My dad made sure I had lunch money. My parents informed me that until my new bus route was in place, I would be picked up at the end of each day. As soon as the principal and my parents left, Mrs. Carson signaled for a girl named Leslie to come to her desk.

"Pumpkin, this is Leslie," Mrs. Carson said.

"Hi, Leslie." "Hi, Pumpkin," Leslie responded. You could hear snickers and giggles from the whole class, especially the boys. "That's enough," Mrs. Carson said sternly. "Oh forget them," whispered Leslie. "I've been picked as your partner. Why don't you hang up your coat over here by mine?" Leslie seemed nice enough. Mrs. Carson gave me a name tag to hang up inside the coat rack. There was a cubby hole for my book bag.

Leslie began to instruct me, "You'll probably want to take your notebook and pencils out of your book bag. Your desk is also beside mine. Come on." I noticed there were five groups of teams. I followed Leslie to our team. Four teams were in groups of four desks. Our team had five. *We had all girls on our team. Great!*

"Challengers, introduce yourselves to Pumpkin and explain the class, as well as the team rules," said Mrs. Carson.

"Hi, I'm Tasha."

"I'm Celeste."

"I'm Stephanie-Rae."

"You know me, Leslie."

"Pumpkin," I said with a half-smile on my face. Then there was this awkward silence. Finally, after each of the girls kept looking at each other, one of them got up enough nerve to ask the famous question. "How on earth did you get the name Pumpkin?" asked Celeste.

Chapter 2

The Challengers

"My mom's favorite color is orange," I explained. "When I was in her stomach my father would talk to me and call me Pumpkin. That's how I got my name." "But isn't it hard having a name like that and having everyone ask you the same question?" Celeste inquired. "Yes," I answered. *I was a bit relieved that this part of the conversation was out in the open.*

I could tell that Celeste was the leader of the pack. She didn't shut-up the whole time Mrs. Carson was writing today's journal lesson on the board. The girls told me how all three fifth grade classes were sectioned off in teams within their own classes. Each team had to come up with their own name. Tasha bragged that I should feel privileged to be a *"Challenger."* No other group was called by their team name outside of the classroom except for them. They also informed me that Mrs. Carson was a cool teacher but that I shouldn't test her patience.

I noticed that Stephanie-Rae didn't speak much, but she was not a push-over. When big-mouth Celeste tried to keep talking, Stephanie-Rae shot her a look of disapproval. Silence was certainly golden. Celeste was heated that Stephanie-Rae had cut her off, but she didn't argue. I got the feeling that I was going to like Stephanie-Rae.

Since most of my morning was spent getting registered into the school, before I knew it our class was walking to lunch. "Here Pumpkin, you can walk behind me, that way I can show you how the lunch room works," Leslie offered. *Did I mention that Leslie was starting to get on my nerves?* I've been to more lunch rooms than the average kid. I think they all basically have the same routine: Follow in line, grab your tray, pick up your fruit and milk, and pay the lunch lady. Leslie started up again, "What you're going to do is..." "Please Leslie, give it a rest," interrupted Tasha. "I think Pumpkin has been in a school cafeteria before." "I know what Mrs. Carson instructed me to do," Leslie replied. "Enough already," hissed Stephanie-Rae. Let's just have a cool lunch so that recess will go smoothly." Stephanie-Rae must have seen the puzzled look on my face because she answered my question before I could ask. "If we have any problems at lunch we cannot play during recess. You want to make Mrs. Carson mad, then act up when she is not around. You want to make her happy, let the lunch monitors give her a good report." "Gotcha," I responded.

The lunch room was crazy. Everybody was talking and chewing at the same time. As kids walked in people noticed their friends but when the Challengers walked in people *really* noticed.

"Hey, Leslie."

"Hey, Tasha."

"Hey, Celeste."

"Hey, Stephanie-Rae."

My goodness! This team is no joke.

I know I would have gotten a "hey" but they had no idea what my name was. "So what are we going to do today at recess?" asked Tasha. "How about play?" *I said it before I thought about it.* I could tell from their looks, that playing was not on their minds. "What? Y'all don't like to play?" I asked. "Sure we do," said Celeste. "It's just that we like to play this certain game," she continued. "What kind of a game?" I asked. "They like to play with people's minds," Leslie revealed. "Shut-up Leslie!" yelled Tasha.

"No, *you* shut up!" exclaimed Leslie. "All of y'all shut-up!" threatened Stephanie-Rae.

"What kind of game?" I asked again. "We pick a boy one day and a girl the next," quipped Celeste. "Today we will pick a girl and she will get all of our attention. It's like she's our new best friend." *I didn't like the meanness in Celeste's voice nor did I think I was going to like playing this game.* "And if it's a boy?" I asked. "Then they pretend they're interested in him," said Stephanie-Rae. "You used to enjoy it Steph," said Celeste. "Yeah-until I saw how it hurt people's feelings," Stephanie-Rae answered. "You're their friend one day and then the next you drop them like a hot potato. That isn't fair at all." "*Everyone* wants to be a Challenger," bragged Tasha. "*Everyone!*" Celeste and Leslie screamed at the same time.

Our class was called to empty our trays and line up by the door to wait for Mrs. Carson. If there was one thing that I was absolutely sure about in my new school, it was that I was not playing that stupid game at lunch and I didn't want to be a Challenger in the classroom or outside of it.

Chapter 3

Recess

I didn't say much when we got back to class. In fact, everyone was on their best behavior. Let's face it, we wanted to go outside and play. Mrs. Carson told us to finish the remainder of our social studies lesson for homework, along with the ten questions at the end of the chapter. She told me I could hand in my questions on Friday and that I could be excused from the test since I was coming into the class during the end of the chapter. That made me the envy of everyone. "Aw, no fair." "Lucky you," my classmates hissed.

You could hear a pin drop as our class walked through the hallway. As soon as those double doors opened up towards the playground, everyone took off in a mad rush. You could hear the roar of third through fifth grade screaming and jumping around on the play equipment. Celeste, Tasha, and Leslie walked with a fast pace and began to search for their next victim of "The Game." Stephanie-Rae grabbed my hand and made me run to the open see-saw before anyone could jump on it. "I kind of figured you didn't want to play that game," said Stephanie-Rae. "Are you kidding?" I asked. My mom would kill me if I played some game like that." Oh no! I didn't mean to leak the "Mommy Rules." I must've really sounded like a baby. I saw the surprised look on Stephanie-Rae's face and she burst out laughing when she saw the look of horror on mine. "Don't feel bad. My mom did kill me" she said. "She found out about 'The Game' when one of the girls went home and told her mother. Then her mom called Mrs. Carson. Mrs. Carson and the vice principal had a meeting with all of us." "Pumpkin seeds! What happened next?" I asked excitedly.

"Our parents received a phone call and a letter. We had to promise never to play 'The Game' again," Stephanie-Rae disclosed. "But you girls, I mean they, still play it," I stated cautiously. "I know, but they lied to their parents," Stephanie-Rae answered. "Are you allowed to say that word?" I asked. "What word?" Stephanie-Rae asked confused. "Lied," I stated. "Oh, that word," Stephanie-Rae continued. "No, but you're not my mom and dad." We both started laughing and I realized I was having a good time getting to know Stephanie-Rae and all the gossip about my new schoolmates. "One more question, Stephanie-Rae," I said. "Shoot," she replied. "Why are you still a Challenger?" "Well, I thought that the girls were going to come clean when we all had our parents notified, but they didn't. I mean they were good for a few weeks but after that, they were up to the same ol' thing. If I told Mrs. Carson that I wanted out of the team, then she would have guessed that nothing changed and I didn't want to be labeled a "snitch."

The whistles blew and each class lined up with their teacher. I loved the second half of the school day. It went extremely fast. Mrs. Carson reminded us of our homework and told the class to relax and wait for the end-of-the-day announcements. As each team waited for their turn to go to their cubbies to retrieve their book bags, I could tell that the Challengers had serious attitudes towards me and Stephanie-Rae. You know how people give you attitude with their body language without saying one word? Like I cared. What a way to start the first day of school! As we headed outside of the building the parents and school busses began to pull into the parking lot. I was glad the day was coming to a close. I had a lot to tell Copper (I'll introduce you to Copper later).

Chapter 4

"Mommy Rules"

My mom couldn't stop fussing about the horrible movers and how they broke her imported crystal, ruined her oriental rug with water damage, and how half of the furniture had a moldy smell. I could tell Dad wasn't having it. He was not about to buy all brand new furniture. He just told Mom to "take it easy" and open all the windows. Tomorrow, he would contact someone and have the furniture cleaned and maybe reupholstered. Mom calmed down and the drive home from school was much quieter.

As soon as we pulled up to our new quarters (that's military talk for housing) I jumped out of the car, ran up the steps and burst through the door. There's nothing like moving to a new place. I can't explain it but I love how my mom surprises me with a makeover in our new housing even though we have the same furniture and linens. As I ran up the stairs my mom yelled that the last room down the hall to the right was mine and that I had better keep it clean. I rushed in and shouted for joy. *"Pumpkin seeds!* Thanks, Mom!"* I yelled down the hallway and woke Elisha up, who was laying in my dad's arms as he was carrying him to his room to lay him down. I mumbled a sorry to my dad and closed the door to my brightly colored magenta, lime green and orange bedroom. My curtains are a lime green sheer with tiny magenta and orange dots. My bedspread is the same shade of green with magenta and orange throw pillows. And sitting right smack in the middle of the pillows is my man, *Copper.* Copper is my twenty-four inch plush teddy bear. Can you guess his color? Copper! Now this is just between us. I tell Copper everything. Yes, *everything.*

"Copper, you are not going to believe my new school. It's so big. My new teacher, Mrs. Carson, is cool so far. She sat me with this team called the Challengers. I figured that it was pretty awesome that I was automatically popular, with being a new student and all, but the girls seem mean-except for Stephanie-Rae. She's my new best friend-I think. Do you think it's okay for me to claim her as my new best friend? We did

exchange phone numbers. Anyway, I promised Mommy I would get better grades and stay out of trouble so I should probably talk to her about this group."

I put Copper back in the middle of the bed, grabbed my book bag and started on my homework at my desk. I tried very hard to concentrate on my work but I couldn't get the Challengers out of my mind. *Time to talk to Mom.* I slid down the hallway in my socks and jumped down our new steps, three at a time. We never had housing with upstairs and downstairs. I just love it.

"Have you lost your mind, jumping down the stairs?" Mom asked. I wasn't sure if she wanted a response. It was probably a rhetorical question. "Sorry, Mom." She gave me a frown and then a slow smile. Mom was still unpacking boxes in the kitchen and stirring the spaghetti sauce as I told her we needed to talk. "What's going on?" she asked. "Well, there's this group at school called the Challengers." It's really a team in the classroom but it has turned into a group of girls-*mean* girls."

I told her about today's events and how my new friend, Stephanie-Rae, wants to get out of the group but doesn't want to be labeled as a "snitch." Mom listened very closely to each word and then she spoke. "Pumpkin, you know how I feel about troublemakers. I don't want you hanging with any grown little girls in school, getting your mind off of your work." *"Grown little girls" is translation for, "they want to be an adult but they're still a child!"*

"Mom, I just got to Memorial Park. I don't want to make enemies already," I pleaded. "Sometimes you just have to make enemies when you stand up and do the right thing," Mom said. "But Mom, I can't just rat people out." "Pumpkin! I didn't raise you to be afraid of the truth. If people are hurting others, than it's *your* duty to do the right thing." *Don't you just hate when your parents are right?*

Dinner was an interesting conversation between Mom and Dad. They were talking about the new neighborhood and the weird neighbors. Dad couldn't wait to get some time off so that he could fix up the front yard. Mom was going to check with the beauty shop on base to see if her job application had been accepted. Elisha was making an incredible mess of his dinner and I slurped down my last spaghetti noodle.

Pumpkin, why don't you help me get some stuff out of the truck?" Dad asked. "Okay," I replied. Mom put the dishes in the new dishwasher-well, new to us because we never had one before. Elisha kept yelling "no!" to himself and slinging his spaghetti on his high chair tray. I followed Dad to the truck and he unloaded some boxes onto the sidewalk. "You were awful quiet this evening," he said. "A little tired, I guess," I pretended. "You sure? If you want to talk about something, here I am. I know it's tough being the new student all the time. I'm sorry you have to keep reliving the same situation." "You don't have to apologize, Daddy." I thought about it for a minute, and then I decided to spill. I told Dad *everything*. I told him how Stephanie-Rae and I wanted to get out of the Challengers but we didn't want to be tattle-tails. I told him what Mom said, too.

"Well Pumpkin, I agree with your mom. She is correct. We did not raise you to be afraid of the truth, but I know how it is to be your age and worried about what your friends might think of you. So remember, there is more than one way to skin a cat!" "Huh?" I asked in bewilderment. *No cats were harmed in this book nor ever will be!*

"It is an old saying," Dad continued. "It means there is more than one way to get something done. Now this is what you do."

Chapter 5

On Time

I apologized to Stephanie-Rae's mother for calling after eight o'clock p.m. I introduced myself to her (over the phone) and told her I was new in town and that Stephanie-Rae had been an instant friend. She was very nice and told us both not to talk too long because it was getting late. Stephanie-Rae jumped on the phone and we talked for at least forty-five minutes. I told her everything my dad told me and we debated about how we would approach Mrs. Carson. After both of our moms threatened to stop our phone privileges, we decided we had better hang up. Stephanie-Rae lived in my housing area but her bus stop was three blocks away, so we agreed to see one another at school.

My mom dropped me off and I gave her and Elisha a kiss and ran inside Memorial Park Elementary. It really *was* a nice school. The main hallway had glass cases which held trophies for the math and science clubs, several community program awards and art done by the students. As I turned the hall I noticed the Challengers. They were talking in their little group but when they saw me they put their heads up. I was about to say hello but Celeste rolled her eyes at me and entered the classroom. The rest of the bratty team followed her. *Ask me if I cared!*

Stephanie-Rae and I were about to blow this whole thing to pieces. As I entered the classroom I put my coat and book bag away. I dropped my homework in the "Homework Bin" and took the rest of my things to my seat. "Good morning," I said to the Challengers. Mom said to be nice to people even if they don't have any manners. My grandma would say, "Kill them with kindness."

"Good morning," said the Challengers with nasty attitudes. Oh, well. I would be just fine when Stephanie-Rae arrived. However, the third bell-which is the late one-rang and Stephanie-Rae still hadn't showed up. Maybe she was running a little late and her parents were going to drop her off.

We said the Pledge of Allegiance, listened to the morning announcements and *still*, no Stephanie-Rae! At this point my blood was about to boil. I just knew after all of that conversation we had that she didn't ditch me and decide to stay home. Well, if she thought that I was going to tell Mrs. Carson about the Challengers and leave her squeaky clean, she had another thing coming. I slammed my pencil down on my desk and everyone on my team jumped. I didn't realize that I had a fight with myself and the whole team was looking at me as if I was going crazy. "Sorry," I said.

"Can I please have everyone's attention, I have some serious news to tell you and we must make some changes immediately," said Mrs. Carson. She waited for the team in the back of the classroom to stop talking. "We have a virus going around the school and a couple of kids in the classroom have become ill. Carlos Vega and Stephanie-Rae Taylor are both at home with high temperatures. The nurse is asking for everyone to please cover your mouths when you cough or sneeze and to wash your hands, especially after you use the restroom. We also have one of our students, Marla Graham, transferring into another classroom within the school. When you see Marla, please encourage her. Now having said all of that, we must make some changes."

Mrs. Carson's class phone rang and she excused herself. The whole class was in a buzz. Stephanie-Rae was out sick and talk about *change of plans*. What was I going to do? I had to think fast. Dad didn't give me a plan "B." Should I continue what we had discussed? Mrs. Carson clapped her hands together and resumed talking.

"Now as I was saying, we must make some changes. Our groups are a bit off. One of our biggest projects is coming up and we have to make sure everything is together before we can begin working on the fifth grade Universal Bowl!" The whole class cheered. I had no idea what the "Universal Bowl" was. I was about to ask Celeste but her and Tasha turned their heads away from me. I looked at Leslie with a smile.

"Oh yeah, that's right, you're my partner. What exactly is the Universal Bowl?" I asked. Leslie looked furious but knew she had to answer my question. After all, Mrs. Carson had assigned her to me. "Every year, each group in the fifth grade classes chooses a state or a country and they have to make a big presentation. Each student does a book report on something specific about your group's state or country. You include your family by making a dish that the location is famous for. You also have to do an oral presentation in front of everyone. The group with the best report gets a prize." "Nice," I commented. "Quiet, please," Mrs. Carson requested. She was talking specifically to Leslie and me. Of course, Leslie had to let her know that it was my fault because

I didn't know what the Universal Bowl was and that I couldn't just wait and listen. I gave her a mean look and Mrs. Carson began speaking again.

"Please let me finish. We need to even out our groups. I'm going to need someone to move to the 'Firebirds' team. I will also need at least two others to move to the 'Bluebirds.'" "Oh no, I'm not moving into those lame teams," said Tasha. "Me either," Celeste protested. "I'm trying to treat you like adults," said Mrs. Carson. Please don't make me choose."

I don't believe it! I could hear my dad's voice. He was right. There is more than one way to get something done. This had to be plan "B." I stood up and raised my hand as high as I could reach. "I'll move, Mrs. Carson," I said politely. "Oh Pumpkin, that won't be necessary. You just moved here and that isn't fair to you or Leslie. After all, she is your partner," Mrs. Carson replied.

"And I'm not moving," yelled Leslie. "That's enough, Leslie. You'll move if I tell you to," Mrs. Carson warned. The whole class burst out laughing and Leslie sat there even more irritated at me than before. I had to get out of this mess. Mrs. Carson thought I was being nice but I really *did* want to move. I had to think quickly.

I looked over at the girls in the Bluebirds who all had a look of horror on their faces. They didn't want a snooty

Challenger to invade their friendly group. That was *it*! We connected with our eyes. They had two people missing from their group. Stephanie-Rae and I could move over there.

"No really, Mrs. Carson. I truly would like to move," I insisted. "And why is that?" Mrs. Carson asked. Celeste was on her feet practically accusing me of insulting her team. I couldn't believe someone I had only known for a day was being this immature. The whole class was looking directly at us and the boys were egging Celeste on. Before I could come back with a sarcastic answer for Celeste, Mrs. Carson interrupted us.

"Sit down, Celeste. I don't know what is going on with this group but I don't like it one bit. Do I need to speak to you young ladies again?" I pretended not to know what Mrs. Carson was talking about. The girls responded with a collective "no" and sat back in their chairs with pouted lips. However, they decided it was best to keep their mouths shut. Mrs. Carson turned to face me. "Pumpkin, why do you want to move?" she inquired.

Think quickly. I can't give her the same sarcastic answer I was going to give Celeste. I haven't even had the time to speak to her in private about the things Stephanie-Rae and I discussed last night. I have to say something. Oh Lord, please help me. Then it came to me. "I can see better up close. I was going to speak to you about it later. Leslie doesn't have to leave the

Challengers to be my partner because Stephanie-Rae said that she would help me if it was okay with you. I figured it would be a good idea since the Bluebirds need two people. I can catch Stephanie-Rae up on our group's project, if you would let us both move. I live near her," I added.

"I don't believe you," said Tasha. "You've just lost recess, Tasha. Put your head down," Mrs. Carson ordered. The class let out a gasp as Tasha was disciplined and she lowered her head onto her desk.

"You're right, Pumpkin. The two of you *do* live close. That was Stephanie-Rae's mom, Mrs. Taylor on the phone. She said Stephanie-Rae would like for you to bring her homework by if that's okay." "Yes, Mrs. Carson. I can do that," I responded. "Great! Pumpkin, since you're going to bring her work home to her than it would only make sense to put the two of you in the Bluebirds. Please move your desk to your new team. Franklin, can you please move Stephanie-Rae's desk up front? Roger and Kevin, can you please move those other two desks back to the Challengers?" Mrs. Carson asked. All the boys jumped up and did as Mrs. Carson requested. I was so proud of myself and let out a big sigh of relief when Mrs. Carson backed me up with Mrs. Taylor's phone call request. Talk about right on time!

Chapter 5: On Time

Chapter 6

A Breath of Fresh Air

After all the desks were moved, Mrs. Carson said she needed time to think about the changes she would make to the Challengers, but that there would definitely be changes made. Their team was in a buzz! Tasha was finally able to put her head back up but she wasn't allowed to speak. She was also on the verge of tears because she and Mrs. Carson stepped out into the hallway to have a serious conversation. When they came back in Tasha looked furious and Mrs. Carson was in a very bad mood for the rest of the morning.

I, on the other hand, was able to breath. My new teammates were Kelly Martin and Ivy Reynolds. They both were nice and smiled often. Mrs. Carson made our whole class work in silence until lunch. She also told us there would be no recess, which didn't sit well with the class. The Challengers had put Mrs. Carson into a foul mood. Now they were on everybody's hit list. I just hoped the class wasn't angry with me. I decided that now was as good a time as any to see if my new team really liked me.

"Do you guys mind if I eat lunch with you?" I asked. Kelly and Ivy gave me a weird look. Oh, no. I guess they were mad at me-not good when you're the new kid in school. I decided to try and get some pity from them. "I don't think anyone else wants to be bothered with me, especially the Challengers. And to be honest, I don't want to be bothered with them. I mean bothered with the Challengers, not you guys." *I'm nervous.*

"Are you kidding?" Ivy asked. I guess I must have went too far. "We *want* you to eat lunch with us," said Kelly. "Really?" I asked excitedly.

"Yes!" they yelled at the same time. Everyone got ready for lunch and walked quietly in the hallway. When Mrs. Carson left us in the lunch line we all began to chatter away. As I grabbed my tray with a cheeseburger and tater tots, Kelly, Ivy and I went to our table. Kelly spoke first. "Sure, you can eat with us. We are new teammates." With a mouth full of food Ivy jumped in. "You saved our lives. I had just whispered to Kelly that I was not going to work with one of those Challengers. They're troublemakers and

I've been a target of one of their games." "For real?" I asked. "For real," chirped Ivy. "No one is angry at you, Pumpkin. You're actually a hero," said Kelly. "I am?" I asked curiously. "Yes, you are," she continued. "Do you have any idea what those mean girls have done to people in this school?" "Of course not Kelly, she just got here," said Ivy. "Well you know what I mean," said Kelly. "Anyway, they're a bunch of bullies, and I was going to personally tell Mrs. Carson that I'm not allowed to hang out with them inside or outside of school." "Me either," said Ivy.

That was it-bullies! The Challengers were bullies. Kelly and Ivy were cool and we had fun talking to each other at lunch. They were so fired up about the Challengers' nasty attitudes and them ruining everyone's recess that they decided to pull in a few more students and go to Mrs. Carson before lunch was over. I decided that my parents were right. They brought me up not to be afraid of the truth and doing what was best. I was going with them.

Kelly, Ivy and I raised our hands and the lunch monitor came to our table. We told her we needed to speak to our teacher privately about some bullies before the other students came into the room. Kelly and Ivy told me that before I came to Memorial Park, the school had a big review about bullying in school, on the bus and the internet. Anytime this problem arises, it must be dealt with immediately. The monitor agreed to let us go to class and she called Mrs. Carson ahead of time to let her know we were coming down. She told us the other two students who wanted to speak to the teacher had to wait. Only so many children were allowed to leave the lunch room at a time.

I was a bit nervous on our way to the classroom. However, I could feel pep in the steps of Kelly and Ivy. It was almost as if the nervousness was excitement. As we rounded the hallway, the three of us came to a halt and knocked on the door of our classroom. Mrs. Carson told us to come in. "Ladies, what's going on? Ms. Davis said you wanted to talk to me about some bullies?" Ivy spoke first. She told Mrs. Carson about the mean attitudes the Challengers had displayed toward the boys and girls of the fifth grade. She explained their cruel jokes and how they continued to play "The Game" on a daily basis even after they were punished.

Kelly jumped in and told Mrs. Carson how she just got up enough nerve to speak to her today. "I probably would have just continued to take it but Pumpkin inspired me. Here she is the new girl and she had enough guts to stand up to them on her second day of school." I was shocked and proud at the same time. I could not believe what these students had been going through before I had arrived. Mrs. Carson made me practically jump out of my thoughts when she turned her attention to me. "Is this true, Pumpkin?" "Yes, Mrs. Carson," I replied. She stood up and folded her arms across her chest and began to pace around the room and speak to us at the same time.

"I'm so sorry," she said. "Oh that's okay, Mrs. Carson. How would you know if we hadn't told you until today?" asked Kelly. "Yeah, like we said, we wanted to come to you sooner but we didn't know exactly how to approach you without having everyone get mad at us," chimed Ivy. Mrs. Carson began speaking again. "That is no excuse. You should always feel safe, especially in your own classroom. I can't believe those young ladies have wreaked this much havoc. And Pumpkin, I'm so upset you've been apart of something like this on your first two days of school."

"It's not your fault. I just couldn't be apart of their team or games," I said. I felt this would probably be a good time to help Stephanie-Rae get out of her mess as well. "Mrs. Carson, Stephanie-Rae is the one who really protected me. She told me that her parents really came down on her when the Challengers were punished the first time. Stephanie-Rae and I were going to speak to you today about switching groups but she got sick and well, you know the rest." Mrs. Carson began to pace the floor again. The three of us looked at each other in silence. Mrs. Carson was thinking very hard about this whole situation. Finally, she spoke. "I want the three of you to leave everything to me." "But Mrs. Carson, there are other kids in the class that need to speak to you," said Ivy. "I know, and I'll let them have their say. I just need the three of you to be calm and trust that I will have this entire matter taken care of by the end of today. Got it?" she asked. "Got it," we all said.

Mrs. Carson instructed us to go down to the storage room and get some bulletin board paper in the colors of the rainbow to represent the different nationalities of the world. We also had to get different colors of construction paper so that each group could make flags for their selected states or countries and national themes such as birds, flowers, landmarks and so on. The three of us were so excited about Mrs. Carson's secret plan that we couldn't think straight. Ivy and Kelly told me that our country would be Jamaica. Ivy would write about the history of Jamaica. Kelly's report would be on the agricultural production of the country. Stephanie-Rae would write about famous people from Jamaica and I would write about the tourism of the country. Each group had to do an art project pertaining to their topic. I figured I'd make a replica of a hotel resort. After my group and I returned to class with the new supplies we all quieted down because the morning had been just awful.

"May I please see the 'Jayhawks' in the hall?" Mrs. Carson requested. "I suggest the rest of you work quietly on your reports." Now when have you ever known a class to be quiet when your teacher steps in the hallway? Every group looked at each other and began whispering in their own groups about what Mrs. Carson was speaking to the Jayhawks about. "Kelly, what do you think she's asking them?" "How should I know, Ivy? What do you think Pumpkin?" Kelly asked. "I don't know, but whatever it is she sure didn't look happy," I commented. "You got that right," said Kelly.

After ten minutes or so, we heard the door creak open and we all delved into our lesson. "May I please see the Firebirds and no talking Jayhawks," Mrs. Carson said sternly. The Jayhawks jumped into their lesson before we could question them. We all spoke to each other with bugged eyes and decided not to make another sound. I couldn't help but look over at my old team. They were nervous, very nervous.

The door opened up and the Firebirds went to their seats. Next, Mrs. Carson called the "Bookworms" and then our group, the Bluebirds. She asked if we had anything to add to our story from lunch and we told her that we didn't. My stomach was churning! We went back into the classroom and then Mrs. Carson made her ultimate move. Pumpkin seeds!

"Challengers, in the hall," ordered Mrs. Carson. She

stayed in the hallway so long with the Challengers that we figured she had just forgotten us. Finally, the door opened up and it was Mr. Hollenbeck, one of the gym teachers. "Good afternoon," he said. "Good afternoon, Mr. Hol-len-beck," we all sang. "Mrs. Carson is busy with a group of students so I will be your substitute for a bit. Now, she said that you all had a rough morning so you cannot have recess outside but I have to make a few personal phone calls so if you promise to stay within your groups I'll let you talk. Deal?" he asked. "Deal," we said.

Mr. Hollenbeck grabbed the class phone and took care of his business while we all conversed with one another. Franklin was the first from the Jayhawks to admit that Mrs. Carson was fed up with the Challengers and that she wanted to know everything that had occurred. After his confession the whole class began to discuss the questions Mrs. Carson had asked in the hallway and the cruel games the Challengers had inflicted on them personally. Franklin, however, swore that the girls never caught him in "The Game" because Celeste had a crush on him. Yeah, right! Well, he is kind of cute.

Anyway, from one thirty until two fifteen we had the time of our lives. As we were chatting away, another call came in on the class phone and Mr. Hollenbeck told us to, "Zip it." "Hello, Mrs. Carson's class. Yes, Mrs. Fletcher. I sure will. No problem. Thank you." Mr. Hollenbeck hung up the phone and I don't think any of us breathed after we heard him mention the principal's name. "That was Mrs. Fletcher. She said that Mrs. Carson is busy in her office with some parents. You are to take your unfinished morning work home and continue working on your Universal Bowl project." We really didn't hear much after "busy in her office with some parents," because "Ooohh," was all I heard from everyone including myself. Boy, I couldn't wait to get home to tell Copper and Stephanie-Rae.

Chapter 7

The Right Thing

As Dad and I were walking out of the school, he gave me a hug and I grabbed his waist as hard as I could and gave him the biggest grin I think I've ever smiled. "Wow, what was that for?" he asked. "Dad, did you forget what we talked about last night?" "No way, I've been thinking about it all day. How did it turn out?" he asked. "Awesome! You won't believe this but everyone in the whole class told on the Challengers today. They have been harassing people all year long." "Really?" Dad asked. "Really," I responded.

We got in the car and buckled our seatbelts. Dad had a cold soda waiting for me with lots of ice, just the way I like it. "Thanks, Dad." "Uh-huh," he said as he sipped his drink. "By the way, where are Mom and Elisha?" "Elisha is at Fort Jake's day care and your mom was called in for an interview," Dad answered. "Great, I hope she gets it." "Me too, she's driving me crazy about getting new furniture," said Dad. We both laughed and I finished telling him about the day's events. Dad told me he was very glad everything worked out and that telling the truth was always the right thing to do.

"Pumpkin, promise me something," Dad requested. "What is it, Dad?" "No matter what happens, whether you do something wrong or one of your friends might get into some trouble, never be afraid to come and tell your mom and myself. We are here for you and you will only make things worse when you hide and don't tell the truth. I don't even care if you're at fault. Please come to us, okay?" "I promise, Dad." "Good," he said. "I love you, Daddy." "I love you too, Pumpkin."

Dad showed me where his new company was as if I could remember how to get from one street to another. We decided that we would have Chinese for dinner because Dad ate the leftover spaghetti for lunch and Mom would probably be tired after her interview. To pass some time before we met Mommy, Dad and I picked up Elisha from day care and pre-ordered our dinner. We went to the post's Main Exchange. It's like a big department store for military families. The Main Exchange at Fort Jake was huge! It was like a medium-size mall. It had a couple of eateries, dry cleaning, gift shops, barber shops and a lovely beauty shop. Mom was just finishing up talking to this lady with the biggest french roll I had ever seen. *I'm sure Mom and I will talk about that hairdo later.* Mom shook her hand and made her way through the crowd of people towards us. "How did it go?" I asked. Mom didn't answer right away. She kissed me first, then Dad and Elisha. "They're going to get back to me," she said. "Aw, Mom." "It's okay. I'm sure something will come up. Besides, they're kind of stingy with their prices and pay," Mom explained.

Let's go eat," said Dad. "I'm too tired to cook. Let's get take-out," said Mom. "We beat you to the punch Mom-Chinese," I said with a smile. "Perfect," said Mom. Dinner was delicious and I couldn't wait to talk to Stephanie-Rae afterwards. Unfortunately, by the time we ate dinner and I took a bath it was close to nine o'clock. It was too late to be calling someone's home on a school night and I had to get to bed in thirty minutes. I grabbed Copper and was about to chat away when the doorbell rang.

I could hear my mom mumbling about who could be at the door this time of the night and since we were new in town, we were really wondering who it was. I tiptoed through the hallway and to the edge of the top step to eavesdrop as my mom opened the door. "Hello, Mrs.

Jackson?" "Yes?" Mom answered. "Hi, my name is Sheila Taylor and this is my daughter Stephanie-Rae." "Oh, yes. Please come in. It is so nice to meet you. My name is Bea, short for Beatitude."

My mom barely got the words out of her mouth before I slid down the stairs in my socks and jumped down the last three steps to greet Mrs. Taylor and squeal at Stephanie-Rae, who looked a little weak but happy to see me, too. "Well this must be Pumpkin, whom I've heard so much about," said Mrs. Taylor. "Yes," Mom replied. Then she looked at me and said, "And child, what did I tell you about jumping down those stairs?" "Sorry, Mom. It's nice to meet you, Mrs. Taylor," I said. "It's nice to meet you too," said Mrs. Taylor, before turning to face my mom. "I do want to apologize for coming by so late. My husband had to go out of town on business so I had to drop him off at the airport. Stephanie-Rae's older sister is away at college so I couldn't leave her home alone. I came by to get her homework because she won't be returning to school until Monday."

"Oh don't worry about the time, please have a seat. I'm sorry we forgot your phone number at home. I had an interview and things just got crazy after that. Sheila, this is my husband Ben," said Mom. "Nice to meet you Ma'am," said Dad. "Oh, please call me Sheila. It's nice to meet you, too." Mrs. Taylor began speaking to Mom again. "You don't have to apologize-I know how it is trying to settle in. If you're sure it's okay I'll only take a minute," Mrs. Taylor said reassuringly.

Daddy told Mrs. Taylor to get better acquainted with my mother and if they would excuse him, he was going upstairs to do some work on the computer. Stephanie-Rae and I held our breath at the bottom of the stairs until her mother said that she could hang out with me for just a few minutes. She said something else but the two of us didn't hear a thing because we bolted up the stairs to my room. "Oh my goodness, I've been itching to talk to you all day, Pumpkin." "I know! I couldn't wait to get home to give you a call but today has just been absolutely crazy," I said. "Talk fast and don't leave a thing out. We haven't got much time," Stephanie-Rae said.

"Okay. It all began when Mrs. Carson told us that you and Carlos Vega were out sick and that Marla Graham would be transferring into another class." "Go on," said Stephanie-Rae. "Well, I had to think quickly! You weren't there to carry out our original plan to speak to Mrs. Carson first thing in the morning. I realized that there were two empty seats in the Bluebirds' team so I offered to move out of the Challengers." "Oh my goodness, I wish I could have seen their evil faces," hissed Stephanie-Rae. "You should have," I said. I told Stephanie-Rae *everything*. I told her how Celeste jumped up out of her seat and accused me of insulting the Challengers and how Tasha got into the most trouble. I told her about how Kelly, Ivy and I talked to Mrs. Carson and how Kelly and Ivy rallied the other students to stand up for themselves because the Challengers were nothing but bullies. "That's *right*. You weren't here Pumpkin, but Memorial Park just had this big workshop for the teachers and students about bullying and how it must be dealt with immediately," said Stephanie-Rae.

"I know-Kelly and Ivy told me. But here is the best part of the whole story!" I screamed. "Pumpkin?" Mom called. "Yes, Mom?" "It's time for Stephanie-Rae to go home," she said. "Here we come," I answered. We both dropped our shoulders at the same time and said, "Aw, man." "Okay, tell me as quickly as you can while we are walking down the hall and the steps," said Stephanie-Rae. "Okay," I agreed. "Mrs. Carson pulled every group into the hallway and told them she knew about 'The Game' and all the other mean things the Challengers were still doing to people. She said that they had to tell her everything that has been done to them so that it would never happen again. And then, the *ultimate*," I said. "What, Pumpkin?" Stephanie-Rae asked curiously. "She called the Challengers into the hallway last and they never returned to the classroom," I replied. "Oh my goodness! Or as you like to say, '*Pumpkin Seeds*,'" said Stephanie-Rae.

We didn't even realize that we were at the bottom of the stairs and that our mothers were standing there with their arms folded waiting on us. We both started laughing and gave each other a hug. Mrs. Taylor and my mom also gave each other a hug and I thought it was going to be the start of a nice friendship between us all. I told Stephanie-Rae that I would get the rest of her homework for her. We waved goodbye and Mom and I talked for a few minutes.

"I really enjoyed Sheila-*Mrs. Taylor* to you, of course," said Mom. "Yes, Mom. I told you that you would like Stephanie-Rae," I said with a grin. "Well, I didn't get a chance to speak to her but if she is anything like her mom than I know she is nice. Mrs. Taylor told me about a few openings at some of the hair salons in the downtown area. I think I will check them out tomorrow. Oh, before I forget, I need you to put this note in your folder right now and give it to your teacher for Mrs. Taylor. It's concerning Stephanie-Rae being out and you picking up the rest of her work," Mom said. "I'll do it right now," I replied. "Give me a kiss and go to bed," Mom said. I kissed her on the cheek and went upstairs. I put Mrs. Taylor's note in my folder and hung my book bag back on the knob of the door. I was just tucking myself in when I heard a knock at the door.

"Come in," I said. It was Mom. "Pumpkin, listen to me very carefully." "Yes," I said. "I'm glad you have found a good friend in class and I know it is not easy traveling from one place to another but I need you to be smart and realize that every day is a learning situation." "What do you mean, Mom?" I asked confused. "Remember that you are in school to learn. You and Stephanie-Rae will have plenty of time to have fun but learning comes first, you understand?" "Yes, Mom." "And most importantly, don't go around bragging about breaking up the Challengers. Just go to school tomorrow, mind your business and keep quiet-that way you don't have to worry about things coming back to you. Do you understand?" "I think so," I replied. "Good night and say your prayers." "Good night, Mom." *What a day!*

Chapter 8

T.G.I.F.

I jumped out of bed this morning with an excitement I could not explain. This has been one of the most stressful weeks of my life. Hey, I know I'm only ten years old but we stress out, too. As I was putting on my clothes my mom yelled up the stairs to me that breakfast was ready and I'd better get a move on. I told her that I would be down soon. I looked at Copper sitting on my bed and realized that I had been neglecting my friend. That wasn't cool at all.

"Hey, Copper. I'm sorry we haven't had a chance to chat. You know things have been pretty crazy around here lately. I promise when I come home today I will tell you all about my adventures in fifth grade. Please be a little patient with me and you will get the scoop."

"Pumpkin? Hurry up girl!" Mom yelled. "Here I come." I rushed to check my book bag. "Social Studies book-check, journal-check, homework in folder and note from Mrs. Taylor- check." I ran down the stairs-softly, I might add. When I walked into the living room to put my book bag down I noticed that Elisha was asleep on the couch and fully dressed. "Mom, where are you guys going this morning?" I asked. "Hurry up and eat your breakfast. And yes, we are going somewhere. Your dad had to get to work early so your brother and I are going to take you to school and run some errands," Mom answered. "Oh, okay. Mom, I'm a little nervous about today," I said. "Did you say your prayers?" she asked. "Yes, Mom." "Then things will work out just fine."

When I finished my breakfast, we packed everything up and loaded Elisha into the car. Mom told me to remember what we discussed last night and I told her I would. She dropped me off and I told her and Elisha that I loved them. As I went into the school I took a deep breath and began walking to my class. As I turned the corner to my classroom, I noticed that most of the class was in the hallway. I asked one of the students what was going on and she said that Mrs. Carson was in the classroom with the principal, and some other man and woman. Kelly and Ivy rounded the corner and immediately made their way over to me. "What's going on?" asked Ivy. "I really don't know. I just got here myself," I said. "All I know is that Mrs. Carson and Mrs. Fletcher are in the room with some man and woman." Our excitement was building so much that the teacher next door told us to pipe it down in the hallway or she was going to call the principal. Franklin told her that Mrs. Fletcher was already in our classroom. The teacher pursed her lips together and closed her door. We snickered when her door closed and the guys gave Franklin a high-five for his snappy comeback. We waited a few more minutes and finally, the door of our classroom opened. Mrs. Carson came into the hallway to speak to us. You could almost hear a pin drop! *Oooh, I wish Stephanie-Rae was here.*

"Good morning, class," said Mrs. Carson. "Good morning, Mrs. Car-son," we all said. "I'm sorry that I had you waiting in the hall for such a long time, but I have a surprise for you this morning." We were all excited, anxious, and curious at the same time. "But hold on. Before you get too excited, this surprise may be a little different from what you're expecting," cautioned Mrs. Carson. She must have seen the looks on our faces because we didn't have a clue as to what she was talking about. "Just come into the classroom and quietly put your coats and book bags on the back of your chairs. Our visitors don't have long with us."

We all did as Mrs. Carson instructed us to do. Mrs. Fletcher was standing in front of the chalkboard with our two visitors. When we all got settled in, Mrs. Carson nodded her head to Mrs. Fletcher. Mrs. Fletcher began to speak very rapidly. "Good morning, students. First of all, I want to personally apologize for the abuse that some of you have suffered at the hands of three young ladies. I was truly shocked when Mrs. Carson came to me on yesterday, to inform me that this group has been up to no good again. To advise you of just how serious this is, I will be sending a letter home to each and every one of your parents to inform them of what has happened and to meet with them as a group. I also want you to know that all three young ladies have been suspended from Memorial Park Elementary and when their suspension is over, they will each have to attend separate schools." We sat there in amazement and I don't think I even breathed. *Wow, pumpkin seeds!*

Mrs. Fletcher continued speaking. "Now, I would like to introduce you to two special people. This is Mr. Preston, our Superintendent. This is Ms. Charlotte. She is a social worker at the Fort Jake Health and Wholeness Community Clinic. At this time I will let each of them speak." Mr. Preston stepped forward to speak first. He apologized as well and promised that he would do his absolute best to monitor the behaviors of the Challengers and other bullies within the school district. Ms. Charlotte spoke next. She was a small lady with a strong voice that captured our attention. She explained how she does seminars throughout New York and sometimes in the surrounding states for school employees and students concerning mental and physical abuse. She explained that bullying is a form of abuse and that she was overjoyed that we stood up as a class to confront this problem. She also said that in some districts the Challengers could and would be considered a gang! She reiterated that this type of behavior must be dealt with right away.

Ms. Charlotte had some booklets for us which included information about friendship, respect, school cliques, and signs of bullying. Each booklet had a free telephone number on the back that was available 24/7 and it promised that whatever we called to talk about would be kept private. Ms. Charlotte asked if any of us had questions. One girl in our class named Melissa, wanted to know if the Challengers would seek revenge on us. Mr. Preston stepped forward to address Melissa's question. He assured her and the whole class that these young ladies were in big trouble. Not only were they being punished but their parents were reprimanded for their daughters' actions. Mr. Preston said he believed the Challengers didn't realize just how serious of a problem they created. He hoped that this experience would change their way of thinking in the future.

Ms. Charlotte answered a few more questions from other students. She told us that the Challengers and their families would have to seek counseling to deal with the emotional wounds that they created. She also said that she would return to speak to us and our families in the coming weeks since we may have emotional wounds that we don't realize exist. Finally, Mrs. Carson stepped forward. "I am so proud of the way you all have sat here so attentively. I know that it has not been easy for you, but because of your honesty I am proud to announce..." She hesitated, and the whole class leaned forward in our seats. "...That Mr. Preston will pay for our class to have a pizza and bowling party at Wilson's Bowling Lanes after the Universal Bowl!" *Pumpkin Seeds!* We went crazy. We were jumping up, cheering and giving each other high-fives. "Hold on everyone, please calm down," Mrs. Carson requested. We were so excited that we didn't even recognize that she was trying to calm us down. "I know that you are very excited but there is an exception to this party," Mrs. Carson alerted us.

Some of the students began to moan but I quickly remembered what my mother and I had spoke about last night and decided that a party was a party. I was going to be thankful and curious in a very quiet way-even though my insides were screaming. Mrs. Carson cleared her throat and the class quickly quieted down since our principal and special guests were only a few feet away from us. "Children, *please*," Mrs. Carson requested. "Now Mr. Preston decided that you should be rewarded. However, your party should be a learning experience as well. When the date is set for the bowling party you will partner with Ms. Freehold's kindergarten class. Their class's field trip was cancelled last month due to a thunderstorm. The four of us want you to set an example of how older children should treat younger children."

"May I interrupt Mrs. Carson?" asked Mr. Preston. "Oh yes, Mr. Preston," she responded. Mr. Preston began to explain the reasoning for our class to partner with the younger students. It never hit me until he began to speak and walk at the same time that he was a very tall man with reddish-brown hair. He also had freckles across the bridge of his nose. *Sorry, Mom is always telling me about daydreaming.* "So you see children, just because someone didn't treat you with the respect that you deserved, I don't want you to display that attitude towards others," Mr. Preston continued. "I want you to set an example for Ms. Freehold's class. This will be fun but most of all it will be a wonderful learning experience and perhaps the start of something new in our school district." Mrs. Fletcher had us to thank Mr. Preston and Ms. Charlotte for coming to speak to us. She also reminded us that letters would be sent home to our parents informing them of everything that had happened and the upcoming date of our party. Mrs. Carson walked our guests into the hallway and we all began to speak at once.

"Can you believe that-we got to party with the kindergartners," Ivy said with her hands on her hips. "Who cares," said Kelly. "As long as we get a day off of school I'll party with the *Pre-k*." The three of us burst out laughing. Mrs. Carson came back into class and quickly had us hang our coats and book bags up. After each team put their overnight work into the homework bin, I realized that I hadn't given Mrs. Carson Mrs. Taylor's note for Stephanie-Rae. I walked over to Mrs. Carson's desk and handed her the note. "Thank you, Pumpkin. Just let Stephanie-Rae know that the only homework for the weekend is to start a rough draft of her report on Jamaica for the Universal Bowl. It doesn't have to be finished but I *do* need to see the direction in which she is going." "Yes, Mrs. Carson," I replied. "As a matter of fact, let me get all of you started on this right now," Mrs. Carson said.

She quieted the class down and gave us instructions on how to do our rough drafts. Mrs. Carson said that she wanted the whole class to do their absolute best on their individual projects. "You have three weeks until the due date. Please don't wait until the last minute. Remember, we are inviting any parents that don't have to work. You don't want to look unprepared in front of our guests." There was so much excitement about this event. I couldn't wait to get started on my model of the hotel resort but I knew that I had to write the rough draft about Jamaica's tourism first. Boy, I tell ya, "T.G.I.F." (Thank Goodness it's Friday) was becoming "T.M.I." (Too Much Information).

Chapter 9

The Universal Bowl

P umpkin get a move on!" Mom yelled. "I'm coming," I answered. This is the big day-the Universal Bowl! All the fifth-graders and their families have been working very hard. My replica of the island resort came out great. Dad spent $138.45 on all of the art supplies. He has reminded me every single day for the past three weeks. Every time that I asked for some extra money he mentioned the "$138.45." I probably won't see an allowance for the next eight months.

"Well Copper, this is it. I'm so nervous. I hope we take first place! I'll fill you in later. I gotta go."

I grabbed my book bag and zipped down the hallway and stairs. Mom was in the kitchen and Elisha was in his high chair eating toast with jelly. "Mom, where is my resort?" I asked with a shaky voice. "Your dad boxed it up and put it in the back of the truck-and good morning to you, too," Mom said with a hint of sarcasm. "Yes!" I exclaimed as I clenched my right fist, pulling my arm back in celebration. "I'm sorry, Mom. Good morning to you and Elisha." She smiled and blew me a kiss. "Now eat your cereal and toast." "I'm too nervous to eat. How do I look?" I asked.

The attire for the day was a t-shirt and jeans. We had a choice of three colors for our shirts: light blue, white or black. Our team chose black with the Jamaican flag and the words, "Jamaica Mon" printed on the front, which were made by Kelly and her mom. Kelly's family was from Jamaica so she was extra proud of her work. On the back of each of our shirts was the subject assigned to us. My shirt said, "Tourism Mon." "You look just fine," said Mom. "Now, eat. There is no way that I'm going to have you passing out in the middle of your presentation." "Yes, Mom," I said with a big smile. As I ate my food, all I could think about was how this past month flew by so quickly. I finished my breakfast and began to put Elisha's coat on him as Mom ran outside to warm up the truck. I double and triple-checked everything concerning my report: written report-check, 3-by-5 note cards-check, hair pulled up in a bun with kyrie shells pinned around in a circle-check. "Sweetheart, get out of that mirror, you look fine," Mom said reassuringly. "Now let's *go* so I can drop your brother off at day care and get a good parking spot at the school." "I don't think I can breathe," I said in a serious tone. My mom rolled her eyes at me and we loaded Elisha into his car seat. I looked in the back of the truck just to make sure my hotel replica was back there (hey, you never know, Dad could have made a mistake and taken it to work in the other car) and it was. We dropped Elisha off and were on our way. Mom was giving me some oral report tips when her cell phone went off. She clicked her Bluetooth and began to talk. It was Mrs. Taylor, Stephanie-Rae's Mom. I could hear Mom telling her that she would love to sit by her in the auditorium and that we would be pulling up to the front of the school in about ten minutes or so.

I was trying to calm myself down. Each group would have to stand on stage before all the parents and the fifth grade classes. There were about thirteen groups. Each group had fifteen minutes to present their work. Each student had to turn in their personal handwritten work to their teacher before reporting to the auditorium. If anyone in your group didn't turn in their report, it automatically disqualified your group from entering the contest for the prize but you would still receive an individual grade.

I was so glad that we had left home extra early. We saw Stephanie-Rae and her mom walking toward us as we parked the car and got out. Stephanie-Rae and I began to hug and squeal while our moms hugged one another and shook their heads at us. "Bea, if Pumpkin's hotel model isn't too heavy I can help you carry it in and the custodians will put it on a cart and wheel it to the auditorium for us," said Mrs. Taylor. They already have a table set out in the hallway with the art projects waiting to be transferred." "Sounds good to me, Sheila. Then the girls can get a move on to class," Mom replied.

We were so excited. I double checked to make sure my replica had its identification card glued down on the foundation board. I grabbed my book bag and Stephanie-Rae and I helped our mothers pull the box out of the trunk. By the time we began walking up the sidewalk towards the front door, more parents and students began to arrive. A man saw my mom and Mrs. Taylor carrying the box and offered to help. My mom and Mrs. Taylor both thanked him for his help and sent us off to our classroom. Just as we were walking down the hall Ivy and Kelly came running towards us. They told us that their moms wanted to meet ours so we turned around and introduced our mothers to the girls. Kelly explained that her mom had printed extra t-shirts for the parents to wear to match our group. Mom and Mrs. Taylor thought that was the sweetest thing and agreed to go meet the ladies in the auditorium. They told us to hurry up and get to class.

As we entered the fifth grade wing there was a sea of blue, white and black t-shirts with birds, flags, states, countries and even food printed on them. It was so cool to look at everyone's hard work and imagination come to life. Our teachers were just as excited as we were and decided to give us extra time in the hallway to talk to students from other classes and comment on each other's work. There was such an air of positivity that I was having conversations with students that I didn't even know. The third bell rung and we all began to assemble in our individual classes. After the pledge and morning announcements, Mrs. Carson began to collect all written assignments. As she went down her checklist she held her head up with a smile. "Good job, all reports are accounted for," said Mrs. Carson. The whole class clapped and cheered for one another. "Now, here are a few 'house' rules. Please make sure you have all of your information cards, extra folders for notes, et cetera. No one is to make fun of anyone's report. You will be removed if you misbehave. Please show good sportsmanship and remember that you represent your family, teacher and your school." "Yes, Mrs. Carson," we all said. "Now let's line up," Mrs. Carson ordered.

As we began to line up, Kelly, Ivy, Stephanie-Rae and I began to go over our last-minute details. "Stephanie-Rae, you have your notes on the famous people?" asked Ivy. "Yes," Stephanie-Rae replied. "My hotel replica is already in the auditorium," I said. "I have my history notes," said Ivy. "I have my agricultural notes and the PowerPoint presentation is ready!" said Kelly.

"PowerPoint presentation?" we all asked in bewilderment. "Oh yeah, my dad didn't like the way I had my information on the different card boards. He told me it would take up too much time from our presentation. And since we only have fifteen minutes, he helped me put everything on PowerPoint." "Wow, Kelly! I think we are going to win!" yelled Ivy.

Chapter 10

The Winner Is...

As the classes began to assemble inside the auditorium, the parents began to shout, clap and cheer for their children. We were so amazed at the uproar of the crowd! Then Mrs. Fletcher went up on stage and told the crowd to give an even louder cheer for the "soon-to-be graduating class of Memorial Park Elementary" for all of our hard work and perseverance. The parents stood up and cheered even louder than before. We, the Bluebirds, finally spotted our moms. They looked so cute with their matching t-shirts on. We waived to them enthusiastically and took our seats.

After the introduction of teachers in the very front row, and the judges' panel, made up of parents and community leaders, Mrs. Fletcher yelled, "Let the Universal

Bowl begin!" Presentations were made in alphabetical order. Alaska came first and their team had on light blue t-shirts with an Alaskan Glacier printed on the front. I really liked how they spoke of the endangered wildlife and showed pictures of the polar bears. We were getting nervous because Indonesia was presenting. Mrs. Fletcher stood up and announced, "From Mrs. Carson's class, the Bluebirds, presenting Jamaica!" Once she said that, our moms stood up and cheered so loud that the four of us looked at them like they were losing it! Mrs. Fletcher spotted them in the crowd and acknowledged how wonderful they looked in the team's matching t-shirts.

As we went on stage I began to look into the crowd for my mom. I'm not ashamed to tell you I was as nervous as could be. Mom waived to me and gave me a "thumbs up" signal. I smiled at her and my teammates. I went over to my model and stood by it as Ivy introduced Jamaica and its history. Next was Kelly's turn. She stood aside as the large screen dropped from the ceiling and boy, were the crowd and judges impressed! The lights dimmed and the PowerPoint presentation of Jamaica's agriculture began. Towards the end of Kelly's presentation she surprised Stephanie-Rae by explaining to the crowd that some of the famous people from Jamaica that Stephanie-Rae was going to speak about were about to pop up on the screen. Kelly nodded to Stephanie-Rae to begin and off she went.

One of the judges held up the three-minute sign during our presentation. Stephanie-Rae took another thirty seconds and passed it off to me. I pushed my cart of the hotel replica to the middle of the stage and began to speak about the tourism of Jamaica. I asked Ivy to spin the cart in a full circle so the audience could see the entire project. We had sixty seconds left. We hurried and put the cart to the side. The three of us let Kelly, our team leader, speak for us as we stood beside her with our left hands on our hips and our right legs extended out to the side.

"We, the Bluebirds, would like to thank each of you for listening to our presentation and we would like to thank our teacher and parents for all of their help. As a proud native of Jamaica, I hope that you will visit my homeland someday. To all of you we say..." We counted to ourselves, 1...2...3...and then with a loud voice and the wave of our right hands, "Thanks! Jamaica, mon!" The audience loved it and we began to jump up and down and hug each other. Ivy began to cry and then the rest of us followed. She whispered to us that we were very special to her and we gave each other a big group hug, wiped our tears and left the stage. We breathed a huge sigh of relief and sat down and showed respect to the other teams. Kentucky, Liberia, London, Madagascar, Poland, Senegal, and so on until the last country...you guessed it-Venezuela. Okay, maybe you didn't but that was the final report.

As the last team walked off stage everyone stood on their feet and applauded. Mrs. Fletcher stated that the judges would need a few minutes to deliberate. The panel stepped out into the hallway for about fifteen to twenty minutes. There was so much chatting going on that we didn't even realize that the judges had come in until applause came from the back of the auditorium and steadily moved toward the front. Mrs. Fletcher came back on stage with all the fifth grade teachers. The custodians had rolled up a huge cart with three large plaques ranging from largest to smallest. Each plaque represented first, second and third place Universal Bowl awards. Each winning team would receive their team name and individual names printed on the name plates to be attached to the plaques later on. They would be placed on the "Winning Wall of Fame" in our school hallway. There were also three sets of small trophies on the cart, representing the individuals on the winning teams.

Mrs. Fletcher grabbed the microphone and all three fifth grade teachers held each others hands and wished one another good luck. Mrs. Fletcher spoke and we stopped breathing for a moment. "It gives me great pleasure to be a part of this wonderful event each year," she began. "Come on with it already," groaned Kelly. "I just want each and every one of you to be proud of the great effort and sportsmanship you all have displayed. I am very proud to be your principal," Mrs. Fletcher said. There was more applause from the audience. *Now, come on with it already. I'm anxious.* "Now, for the moment you all have been waiting for. In third place for Most Unique Country and Report, the 'Brain Seekers' from Mr. O'Shea's class, presenting the Island of Cape Verde!" Mrs. Fletcher exclaimed. We all cheered and Mr. O'Shea was so overjoyed. The team ran up on stage and gave him the biggest hug. The photographer snapped their picture with their trophies in hand and they were led over to the left side of the stage to wait for the next two teams to be announced. Our group was squeezing each other's hands and praying at the same time. "Next, I would like to announce the second place team-and might I add in all my thirteen years at Memorial Park this has been the closest race between second and first but nevertheless-for Best Cohesive Teamwork and Use of Technical Support, the Bluebirds from Mrs. Carson's class, presenting Jamaica!" I don't think we heard anything past "the Bluebirds." Actually, I don't think we'll ever be able to hear again, because we screamed so loud that Mrs. Fletcher had to tell us to hurry up and come on stage. Through tears and hugs we ran on stage, grabbed our trophies and kissed Mrs. Carson. I could only imagine what our picture was going to look like. Finally, Mrs. Fletcher announced the moment we all had been waiting for. "In first place for Best Overall Presentation, let's give a wonderful cheer to the 'Philosophers' from Mrs. Davis' class, presenting Hawaii!" They went bananas and they had every right to. They looked fantastic in their white t-shirts with the vibrant colors of the state's hibiscus flower on them. Kelly said that Lela Kanoi was from Hawaii and of course, she had the inside track on how to do a fabulous presentation of her beautiful home state but we told Kelly that she had done a marvelous job for us as well.

Mrs. Fletcher gave her closing remarks. The entire auditorium stood up and gave everyone a standing ovation. Mrs. Fletcher advised the guests to report to the playground where a huge reception tent was waiting for them to enjoy the variety of dishes that they helped their children to create. We, the students, had to first return to our classrooms to put back our notes, models and any other materials we had from the Universal Bowl. We signaled to our moms that we would see them outside. As we entered our classroom, Mrs. Carson had the whole class give us another hand for a job well done. "I'm truly proud of the whole class," said Mrs. Carson. "Thank you, Mrs. Carson" we said in unison. "Now Bluebirds, you are more than welcome to leave your trophies in the classroom which will be locked up but since your parents are here I would advise you to give the trophies to them to take home for you," Mrs. Carson suggested. We decided to take them to our moms.

The classes began to make their way to the playground blacktop for the reception. There was a huge buffet table with everyone's food placed on it to sample and enjoy. There was soda, juice, and water placed at a drinking station and tables and chairs for everyone to relax. Our moms were already seated and eating. We made our way over to them. They were so proud of us and showered us with hugs and kisses. "I hope you don't get mad at me Pumpkin, but I was so excited that I texted your dad about your team winning. Then it occurred to me that you may have wanted to tell him yourself," said Mom. "Oh, that's okay, Mom. Was he excited?" "Girl, he is so proud of you! He just might stop reminding you about how much money he spent on your art project." We looked at each other and said, "Nah."

"Is Fort Jake looking a little better for you?" Mom asked. "Yes Mom, it is." "Good. Only God knows the great things in store for us Pumpkin," Mom said cheerfully. "Yes, and I can't wait to see what is coming next!" I shouted.

The End

Made in the USA
Lexington, KY
05 July 2015